Of Lips and Lashes

By

Emily Armanios

K̶manios

Kira Armanios Email: Karmanios@gmail.com

Cover Design Artwork by Emily Armanios.

Made using Notegraphy. www.notegraphy.com. Design by Mek Frinchaboy. www.holamimi.com

Typesetting by Kira Armanios

Books may be purchased by contacting the publisher at the above email address.

National Library of Australia Cataloguing-in-Publication entry

Creator: Armanios, Emily, author.

Title: Of lips and lashes / Emily Armanios ; Kira Armanios.

ISBN: 9780994520708 (paperback)

Subjects: Emotions--Poetry.
Australian poetry.

Other Creators/Contributors: Armanios, Kira.

Dewey Number: A821.4

For my family, my friends,

and the one that keeps the inspiration burning.

Table Of Contents

Table Of Contents cont...

Table Of Contents cont...

INTRODUCTION

Of new beginnings!
Of fists and fights!
Of tired toasts,
And boastful nights!

Your hand in mine,
A long lost flame—
—I'd like to start
All over again.

THE SOCIAL MONSTER

I am a social monster,
of you I'll take a bite.
I feed on praise, live in a daze,
with things that break the night.

Your words will fuel my appetite,
for love and lust and fame.
I *don't* want to get in a fight—
I want to hear my name.

THIS WINDOW OF OURS

Our foggy window isn't clear,
and though it's still a window, dear,
let's lay back and disperse the fear,
and speak words never insincere.

This glass is fragile — quick to break
a tragic tale this heart can make.
So grin real wide; enjoy the ride!
And savour all that chocolate cake.

This ledge to rest your weary chest,
a trunk with mem'ries put to rest.
They'll never seem to sparkle less,
it's you I want — you *are* the best!

UNTOUCHED TERROR

In thy unkindness,
shaken—beauty hath not seen
terror in thine eyes.

CANDY-CANE HEALER

Our fingers interlock,
like two stray candy-canes
at the bottom of the sweets bowl.

Mint and strawberry stripes
running down our spines.

And just as sweet,
and just as bitter,
and naturally,
with each bite better.

UNKNOWN ERROR UNKNOWN

I remember when we were young and feared nothing.

I don't say fearless because that's not what I mean.

And though we're still young and we still fear something,

the unknown is far scarier under the seams.

EMERGED

I woke up coughing and spluttering your name,
as if emerging from that pool of rest
and finding my gills turned back to lungs—
and finding I never had gills at all.

HEARTBURN

We drove along a bumpy road,
don't say you told me 'cause I know.
We hit a rock — you told me so
and once best-buddies turned to foe.

Don't sing our song, the way it goes,
I know just how and where it flows.
The CD jumps and skips at *'love'*
I find it funny. Ah hah ha.

Don't cook our food, it hurts too much,
you taught me how to bake and such.
Your words still on my birthday cake.
I smudge them. I hate birthday cake.

Don't drink our wine, I just can't bear,
to think of you all perfect there.
Your lips still on the bottle's lid
while lips upon my temples hid.

SUMMER'S CALLING

'Cause she won't wait for any other,
when Summer calls for curls and colour.

If she wants a drink and then another,
she'll down it like a liquid lover.

'Cause she won't wait for any other—
a whole new world
left undiscovered.

BASS DREAMS

I turned off the radio,
sat down in the dark.
The bass of the stereo,
the grace of the mark.

I pretend that I'm not rusting;
forget. Forgive.
It's hard when you are lusting
for a life you'll never live.

SIREN SONG

Is there anybody out there,

who's feeling naught at all?

Is there somebody that's out there,

who's almost blending with the walls?

I can't find home,

although I tried.

I really did,

I really cried!

The solace that I saw in you

was just another siren song.

JUST WHISPER IN MY EAR

If you say my name right here,
I'll make my love shine clear.
Don't speak too loud—
we're not allowed.
Just whisper in my ear.

RIVERS

A dry trench filled with dust and debris,
homesick leaves float south with glee.
He could smile, he could try—
could care, if he pleased.
But care he does not,
nor feel the sweet breeze.

A thousand tears upon the dirt,
he feels the fears, the sky, the earth—
—he chooses not to feel the hurt.
He would be one,
a newfound birth.

With burning rays,
he sits alone.
Those wistful days,
all on their own.

He wants to stay;
and call it home.

EPIPHANY

Maybe one day you'll see—
if you mean anything to me,
you mean *everything* to me.

I SWEAR

Palm trees are nice but your palms are warmer.

I love you and loved you, gave in to the former.

And this wind chills my skin but you got to the bone,

how these things so far away are what I call home.

These sunsets are pretty,

and the sand's oh-so-hot.

But your smile lit the city,

and your name's all I've got.

I swear one day I'll breathe again

to drown in your perfume.

MADNESS DESCENT

I saw you in my dreams

in a mixture of violets,

eggplant,

and amethyst bruises.

WANDERLUSTER

I am looking out the car window,

as the rain drowns out the radio—

making wishes on doorbells

and hoping maybe

one of 'em will come true.

And I am looking out the car window,

at the places I will never go,

and the people I will never meet.

And I think, perhaps,

just one lifetime

isn't enough.

BRAND NEW ADULT

I had so much to teach you,
but I guess you're older now.

Flower in the wind,
your petals are destined for far things,
greater things,
far greater things, in fact.

So stretch your leaves and sharpen your thorns,
and be careful where the wind takes you.

IF THERE IS ONE THING I MUST SAY

We humans have a silly habit
of falling in to where we shouldn't.
And loving while we cause a havoc,
'cause were it not for lust we wouldn't.

But I look at you and see the stars,
the moon pales upon your sight.
I need you whether near or far—
I am a wingless bird in flight.

So lay me down
and tell me lies.
Let me forget
your lilac eyes.

BE PURE

You have mistaken your sorrows for love.
Do not believe, even for a moment,
tender sighs can replace your gaping soul.
Only fools auction off water for wine.

ADAGIO

But people aren't like musics—
that lilt and chime and rock.
Their voices croon and waver,
and spit and stop and lock.

And words are different from the lisps
of superstars and skipping discs.
They melt with care, and felt the flair,
of wonder match the quiet lips.

So don't tell me that I'll meet someone
with music in their veins.
Lest I be swallowed whole and still
and baked live by the flames.

SLEEPWALKER

All my life to now has been a series of events to you.
Like a *turning point.* Before and after; a defining moment
that changes a person.

I wanted to give, you wanted to take,
like a fast-spreading potion with the sweetest of tastes.
And after you leave, I'm dizzy and then,
I just march through the days 'till I see you again.

PALE PRIZE

You've asked me what the woman is enchanting there
with her dripping crimson mouth?

Perfuming from the bony glass, crystallizing the
momentum of her fountain full of tiredness—
a lethargic flower's sleep!
Nothing but that afternoon of daises,
a melancholy poppy day.

Inside the divisions like graphite,
your flower is a bottle filled with decadent kiss,
as if to coagulate or magnify or dig up.

And around my hammock, in the sunrise,
I woke up reddened and full of wonder.

HIGH SCHOOL SWEET HEART

I planted you, my pumpkin seed,
I wanted just a pumpkin tree.
I stole a branch of silken sweets,
I stole your branch; I took, I eats.

FEELING

when your arm is around me and you grasp my hair.

oh my

my hair...

please don't tear

it out.

please don't bite into my flesh or lick up my blood,,don't drink my tears

Actually;;

Please do.

DELIRIOUS DESIRERS

Two tall figures.

Both pairs of eyes lovely enough to get lost in.
But killers in disguise; stalking slow.

Fatal in every language, since
you cannot have the roses without the thorns.
The thoughts of your demise; running low.

They know exactly what buttons to press, but that
doesn't mean they'll push 'em.
All muscle and flesh and toothy grins...
"hello, sweetheart"'s and "looking fine"'s,
and words to read between the lines.

Guys like them are always trouble—
but isn't that the point?

SHE'S JUST BEACHY

Hello, little boat!

Are you watching the sand, or

the sun hanging ten?

YOUR LOVE IS MADE OF

Your love is made of wretched things.
I mean it! Always burns and stings.
It catches, hooks, and latches sing,
with curtains drawn that crumple in.

Your love is made of smoky nights!
The windows call and kick the frights.
With bitten ears and hazy sights,
that sparkle like the Northern lights.

Your love is made of honeysuckle,
Rosemary and red lips puckered.
Long lithe fingers; voices chuckle,
you're a rollercoaster without a buckle.

CRYSTAL TEXTS

From: Him

To: Her

I want you back. Love me?

~

You took from me all that you could,

I hoped you would preserve it.

You said that you had wanted love,

if only you deserved it.

YOU

why do you look with your

your whole body and not only your

your eyes?

when you blink I must rebuild my armour so I am not stung by
your glare again.

and again. again. again.

THERE IS A DUSTY BOTTLE IN THE BACK OF THE CUPBOARD

It's sometimes hard to understand
why you won't love me in lips and hands
why words parade like marching bands
but that bottled love is far too bland.

I don't know why you're still so shy—
and even though you cried and cried,
you promised not to say goodbye.

It's okay.

I know your bottled love's a lie.

OCEANS AWAY

And oh, how I keep longing to be

in your arms, drifting; lost at sea.

But you're gone — you've left — and I can't wait for any other.

'Cause baby, we're starving ourselves of each other.

SCORCHED EARTH

We're halfway to Hell,

and everything's swell,

aside from the fact that

everyone can tell.

SOLAR FLARE

You are the most important thing
I have ever set my eyes on...
so forgive me for protecting you
like you're the last star in the galaxy.

MUSINGS

Do you point your feet this way because you thirst or because
you rest?

it's things like this I am left to wonder...

scrabbling for some hidden meaning behind your "hello"s

or the way your laugh pushes both eyes closed.

I swear; I did not mean to analyse,

or tear you up asunder.

will you notice how I keep my breath in time with yours?

how my steps fall flat and rise with yours?

im scared that after so long of walking side by side

you may never grab my hand.

HE SAYS TO HER

You taste like melted caramel,

and smell like broken spices.

So let's forget our sins,

and give in to our vices.

INFINITELY

Doves scatter under the crispness of the sky,
as the Infinite Woman stands.
She treads in the eager morning, content.

Everything is diluted by quiet voices, the salt of the sea,
and piles of bread upon the table.

WANDERING EYE

It's a sinful thing to feel desire,

for one you can't enjoy.

And lest I'm swallowed by the fire,

I still might like this boy.

MY LADY

My Lady does not walk, she glides,

causing walls like waves to part to the sides.

My lady is Grace with a smile so disarming,

Her eyes quickly read you at a state most alarming.

My lady feels love, of this I am sure,

and I crave at the banquet of her sweet temple's door.

My Lady is Peace, and filled to the brim,

with courage and mischief and romantic whim.

My lady is fairer than I've ever seen,

and I as her maiden will serve her as Queen.

CORPORATE LOVER

Blackened heart
and smoky lungs.
Climbing up
the righteous rungs.

She wants all of your words and tongues.

LIBRARY LIFE

Spines cracking in both

the novel and I;

and wincing both times.

A dampened atmosphere,

with words creating worlds

above the heads of every silent explorer.

Each corner of this sphere

is filled with awe,

tea stains,

and a little bit

of light-headedness.

YOU'RE EVERYWHERE

Surrounded by you
in a house full of people, and
from across the room.

I SEE YOU

I see you in the movies I watch.
I see you in the empty space on
the other side of the bed.

I see you in reflections: mirrors, glass,
cutlery—your face haunts me.
I know I shouldn't shy away, but
it hurts to look too long.

I see you in my future; I see you
at the traffic crossing; I see you
underneath the sycamore tree.

I see you at the bottom of my whisky.

I see you in the words I write and I see you in my dreams at night.
I see you resting motionless in our bathtub.
I see you
I see you
I see you

EYES, IN THOUGHT

He had eyes that were bluer than blue,

and that's funny.

To have eyes

that are more

than the colour

they are.

HEARTBEAT ENVY

Your love was always a magnificent thing.
Unforgiving and dense, yet light as a feather.
It was a certain feeling that only *you* could bring,
with hearts sped up and nerves all tethered.

I was gone from the start, already you knew,
I was yours and you were hers.
I know it's not smart, but what I wouldn't do—
to be a person someone prefers.

TIDAL WAVES

Ancient relics,

dusty days.

Kids who relish

in fractal ways.

You are the *moon* to these tidal waves.

POLTERGEIST

I won't ever get tired of you—I can't.

I see you every day, and I when I leave to go back home,

my *heart* hurts

from the very first moment my head passes through

that frame.

A ghostly painting, I am, only recalling

memories between that doorframe and

your room.

Everything else between is faded.

"You walk around like a Poltergeist," they say,

"the pastel woman whose mind is in the clouds".

But it's not—

it's resting on your pillow,

waiting for my body to return.

BEHIND YOUR EAR

How do you have the world behind your ear?

I want it, let me grab it...

I will try, I will try, let me climb you! I will try

and I will fail and I will fall, but let me try, let me try...

some things are worth more

than the blood of a scraped knee.

LOVESICK LIGHTNING

Just the thought of thunder
is enough to make me wander.
And just the sound of rain
is enough to soothe the pain.

Missing you, the burning stops,
the itching yells and twitching drops.

Lovesick shouldn't hurt so good,
and yet, by God, it does.

LITANY

I need you more than I can say,
so break me, take my breath away!

Slurp out my lungs,
drink in my sighs
—I need your tongue
—I need your eyes!

Oh hon, you've made a mess of me,
so darling, baby, set me free.

SIX AND HALF HOURS SPENT ON

There's a few words to be had,

some things that must be said.

A fact to cure the fad—

to trample on the dread.

A school all filled with tulips,

a gun up to my head.

With paperwork like bullets,

I'd rather die instead.

SEARCH OF NOBODY

At what point

do voices on trains

and shadows on sidewalks

become friends?

I've never sought out danger,

but I'd like to love a stranger.

THE FIREFLY

I caught you in the bar tonight,
a firefly in candlelight.

I saw you smile and walk away,
with all the things I didn't say.

Next time though, I'll bring my jar,
I'll capture you and take you far—
across the seas and through the trees
to rest back at the bar.

DRUNK IN LOVE

You tease me of this all the time,
in verses, prose, and metric rhyme—
so I thought for once, I'd turn the tables,
and write about our fumbled fables.

I was nervous, you were loud,
amusing in the way you howled.
And swiftly, without hesitation,
your heartbeat smashed out palpitations.

I hadn't known the effect I'd take,
and wanted you to dance and shake.

But you were drunk, and all that liquor
came back up a moment quicker.
On the floor and on your shoes,
as the beggars played the blues.

CALL TO ARMS

We rise! Take to the sea—the sky's rays are calling!

Wolf howls sprinting through the night—

a careful tale of triumph:

a boy to smite the beast,

a man to smite the boy,

a lass to smite the man—

Hourglasses dripping sand down the counter!

Our time has not come, but soon it be.

We rise! We rise!

And pray the sun does the same.

ONE DAY

One day you'll forget me.

And I do hope it's a sudden thing—

something that hits you painlessly, with shocking precision

instead of slowly eating away

at the bits of flesh I kissed on you.

Even if it wrecks me, I don't want it to scratch you—

and if, one day, you forget my name

leave it where you stand, broken and/or tender.

For someone maybe to pick up again.

DANDELION FLUFF

How many hours, supposed, have I spent:

wishing and wanting for somewhere to vent?

Your eyes as my throne; the travels I went—

to commence the dandelion's main event.

HOMESICK ARTHRITIS

My fingers hurt. I think I get itchy

when I'm away from you too long.

My joints feel disjointed and my hands don't feel handy.

Oh, but I'm dandy.

That's what I tell people when they see me stretch my bones,

I say it helps me tone but really I'm trying

to spread the layer of your touch so thin through the marrow that maybe I'll forget it.

Like some sort of homesick arthritis, except I'm home and it's not arthritis;

I'm sick for the home that circles your arms

and sick for the bones in need of your charms.

IN THE END

Don't deceive, brothers:
snow, fire, sky and monsters,
war and lovers meet.

POKER COMMUNION

The light flutters like usual
but this time it's quicker
and kickstarts my heart
on the way.

And I've never been a dancer
but I have no other answer
for the moves
that I dealt out today.

We were masters of cards,
little binary shards
with the odds in the house where we pray.

GRAVEYARD RAINS

No tears have been shed
along this short grave but I,
with both wounded eyes.

EMPATHETIC

You read about some girl that's crying,

that's filling up a river with tears and you think,

"I've been there, I hope she's okay," and you get angry—

at yourself because you had nobody to feel empathy

for you when you were crying up an ocean.

And it's unfair,

you think, that this fictional being can have your care and

you pause.

And I know that it might seem like you're reading away your
sorrows,

like you borrowed someone else's life to try to fix your sadness,
and it didn't work and now you can't replace it—

I know it's quite the blow, let's face it—

I was meant to be happy,

and you were as well,

but the whole world is hurting

and it sucks you can't tell.

BETRAYAL

Coerced into lechery
and fuelled by the treachery,
I laid myself bare in your hands.

Though it's not an excuse,
I would have made use
of that pretty mouth making demands.

FAMINE QUENCHER

A quaking hunger has befallen this entire city...

feeding the earth with bread-stick arms,

candy-floss hair,

(like Angel threads)

and boxed-chocolate eyes.

Such a hunger had not been seen in years.

With a thirst involving the river of her speech,

and the shore of her ocean-dress

lapping at her ankles.

TERRACOTTA BODY

"You've injured me," she says.
I look her up and down, she's right—
I have. I can see.

There are cracks in her terracotta body
that've been spilling out light,
and I think that's why her smile
has never been bright.

DANCE, DANCE

Now don't you sit or slouch!
You best pull up those pants.
No lying on the couch—
You best get up and dance!

Now breathe and sigh and sway,
and blink towards the crowd.
Then breathe and jump away,
and wink towards the crowd.

And don't you rest a minute!
Your breath so short it pants:
your bones a maze and in it,
a heart that wants to dance.

Now I said: don't you sit back down!
Be careful with your stance.
Their eyes alone could drown
in the beauty of your dance.

RUTHLESS IN RED

I've had my share of heartbreak,
and even had my heart ache—
on both ends of the scale, too,
where loathing comes to rendezvous.

And if it has to be one or the other,
well, now, I think you know;

what exactly I feel like choosing...
you *know* I don't like losing.

Cold hearts rarely crack.

STARCATCHER

I tried catching stars,
but too many were falling.
Threw 'em back instead.

SUGARED

When I see you, surrounded by light;
your cheeks a dark pink and your skin softly bright,
I can't understand how you don't see yourself
in the way that I do — perfection itself!

When you look in the mirror, what do you see?
How do your eyes not fill up with glee?
Your looks are divine; your body—all mine!
Of my poems, your gaze could fuel every line.

AUTUMN LEAVES AND AUTUMN GROUNDS

How those fluttered leaves, even by the least

of these lines, and tongues—in their barren space

still fall? The earth has not missed them, yet they

rejoice at the death of Summer once more.

FIRELOVE

All around me are these thoughts of a confused love.

When did roses become eyes?
And the sun become a touch?
How did flowers bloom to sighs—
I've never thought as much!

And yet, I hold his hand,
like his palm is made of sapphire;
and his kisses are so grand,
like he's sculpted from blue fire.

BODY OF THORNS

Mountains of wreckage

and at the very centre,

a heart beating hard.

LORD, HAVE MERCY

Lord, have mercy, for I sin—
pillaged and plundered and stole all the gin.
The horns on my head are grinning with glee,
how *luscious* the fruit of sinning can be.

Drank all the blood, they called me a fiend;
'till the voices in throats had given and weaned.
But the teeth on my lips couldn't split them no more,
and the teeth on my hips couldn't split them no more.

"Salvation!" They cry.
Bah! Pass me another.
We've got nothing to fry—
except for each other.

So bring out your dead, we'll eat him instead!
We'll make all them angels clutch hard to their heads.
Their wings are so tiny! We'll fill 'em with dread.
Don't beautiful heaven make you wish yourself dead?

REPARATION EMERGENCY

You're damned if you do,

and damned if you don't;

so do the damned thing,

'cause someone else won't.

POWER TRIP

Count the teeth, hunt the hunger,
resist the thought of drifting under.
Warrior-hero, bigger than this,
eclipsing suns in predator bliss.

Skylines could never hold you down,
so steady on and don't you drown.

FROSTBITE

Brightness flashes from behind polar ice eyes.

An illusion of cool glass diffusing my vision.

I have your name

spilling through my melting fingers—

like ice-cream on

a Winter's day.

CUPID'S BOW

Many a maiden hath come by and you,
so silver in wit and sleepless no more;
on par with a scurv' hath taken mine shoe,
hath taken mine bag, ere sent it afore.

And art thou feathers not wet from flight?
I should speaketh quietly for tonight.
A gentlest quiver in thine bow—
who hath no valour enough to throw.

LIAR

"Everything will be different," he promises,

and then sneaks out to be with her,

and the only thing that's different

is the way he pleads he's innocent.

SKIES

"How doth skies fall so sweetly on thy face?"
A million rose-gardens could not compare.
And in thy temper, thou art still as fair,
with those of the angels, tho thou hath more grace.

Untroubled worth dealing, gracious and soft;
but dabbled in trouble, wielding his sword.
I know'st not of heaven's walls, but know:
it's air would match the tender of thy own,
and cast some other day aloft.

For none would ever stay inside,
with that love along the skies.

LUSTRE

Maintenance of fire; you clear out your lungs,

embracing empty hearts but full lips.

Precious like a dragonfly.

Dragon; fly wherever you want to go—

only love can stop you now.

HOW I MISS YOU

I really Goddamn miss you.

I don't mean like usual—I
miss you wholly, like lovers do;
miss you completely, like the sun and the moon.
I miss you uncontrollably, like the ocean to the shore,
I miss you like I missed you always wanting more.

We lay together, until the dawn was interrupted
by the low-hanging clouds of the next day,
the lightbulbs clicking in and out of existence, letting
themselves be known, and then disappearing again.
Like that, he was here, now and then.

I miss you so much I can barely breathe,
and there's nothing left to do but grieve.

LONELY

Ask me my name! Ask me again!
Talk to me, talk to me; I just need a friend!
Been staring at you just waiting to be heard,
Been dying to talk but spoke not a word.

I kept all my syllables real warm in my hand,
just straining to use them—but falling like sand
they slip through my fingers until I've got nothing,
I wanted it all but couldn't stop blushing.

BIRTH OF A SAINT

Humming of cathedral lights:

methodical and low,

and

somehow relaxing.

Perhaps, I could stay in this

quiet hall forever,

so long that the moon reflects my face

into one of the stained-glass windows.

AMNESIAC

There are moments sometimes where I look in the mirror and
think, *"who am I?"*
Like it's not obvious by the face staring back.
I squint at the reflection and feel strange when she squints too—
disassociated from my features, I sometimes forget myself.

But I can never forget you.

Your beauty is insurmountable, and quite often, overwhelming.
I don't mean the way you look, either, though that is a part of it,
since—
True beauty can't help but radiate towards the skin.

I mean the way you are. So pure and so kind.
Never meaning any harm. And your hands... oh, your hands...

Made to make. Create. Heal. Never used for destruction, and
never harnessed without purpose.

So those times of distress when I look in the mirror are trivial,
because when I see your face, and I smile and you smile back,

I know.

"Ah. There I am."

STARGAZE

Take away the flesh—

this special sin seeps to the bone.

Eyes that slow undress;

I yield, breathe.

Impressed!

I love your haunted fingers; curl—

—to find your way back home.

Rosy lips caress; drip, drop:

alone!

KNOWING YOU, STRANGER

I must have known you in another lifetime,

because I do recall how you loved me:

beautifully, and terrifyingly so.

FLUSTERED HEART

Broken plates and broken hearts,
frilly skirts with sugar tarts.
Candy-canes and purple rains—
magic wands and chocolate trains!

My favourite things cannot be listed
so much stuff, I would've missed'em.
But your sweet kiss would steal the show,
and dazzle in its blissful glow.

Your pinkish lips give me a flustered heart.

FURTHER THAN FATE

Empires fall, and then in faith triumph.

I've never been too fond of fate,
it always seemed to strike too late.
But if you told me you preferred it,
baby, I'd be new converted.

HIDDEN WISTFULNESS

It's all I can think about.

It's warm and warm,
and more and more,
and so much flesh
than seen before.

Melding, melting, perfume and cologne,
or perfume and perfume—
or just on your own.

DÉJÀ VU

There was the smoke and the flame and then there was you.

There was the clouds and the rain and there you were, too.

A fire;

a hurricane,

and a sense of déjà vu.

TRAVELLER

Pulsing hits in perfect fields of grey and blue
pertaining between the two—
we stare.

Who is that foreign figure braiding hair?

I will not rest until my journey is complete—
will move until I've worn my feet.

"Keep moving, child," is all that's known,
so nothing but your strength is shown.

ANGUISH EYES

A silhouette found,
in the midst of a battle;
the tale of two woes,
the echo and rattle.

The silhouette found,
no one'd dared to warn it...
so delicate a sound,
not a beast could ignore it.

MISHAP

I fought until the day was gone,
all up until my heart was torn.
And then the night came swiftly after,
to save me strictly from disaster.

I've never fled with all my strength,
and yet for you go every length.

GLUTTON FOR GLUTTONY

I know that you could ruin me
with the soft click of a button.
I know that you could break me,
'cause I'm a sucker and a glutton.

But I don't believe you are that way,
because it's in your blood.
A storm of tears I cried today,
watch out — here comes the flood.

GOING INSANE

How many days has it been,

since I last felt your touch?

Too long, it seems,

too much.

And how long has it been,

since I last felt your body?

A while, it screams,

to no body.

POLAROID SKY

Old memories of us
in the royal lights,
eating shortbread sticks
and flying kites.

New memories of you,
at the dawn of day
With the springtime dew
in which we lay.

I burned all those memories
when you said goodbye;
since you ripped all the stars
from the polaroid sky.

HEARTBREAK VALLEY

I knew he was poison from the start,
but I let him have me anyway.

Maybe I'm just a magnet for awful, gorgeous things,
or maybe it was those shocking sinful eyes;

but I let him open up my world
and fill it with goodbyes.

BRAINDEAD

I shouldn't say this but I will,

I think about you all the time.

And in my dreams, the haze and swill—

loving you's my only crime.

My thoughts are messy, too divine,

a place where shame runs free.

The spell is great—where you are mine

but just not meant to be.

ISOLATION

I saw somebody
sitting alone in the dark—
staring at mirrors.

MOONBOY

Water, wind, and ever-light,
he stalks the moon upon the night.
His shiver haunts the storming sleep,
which in tendrils up his body creep.

No green grass to run across,
only glass but that's the cost.
The moon is close, it's in his fingers,
the white-hot touch that gently lingers.

In the morning, safe and calm,
kept warm in his loving palm,
the moon shines out, kind and bright,
to guide him in the broad daylight.

CHRISTMAS SPIRIT

Pockets spilling out the sides with
a laundry list of things to buy
children screaming,
shrieking, playing,
warm and under tree lights laying.

FIRESTARTER

Bring me back the fire of your heart.

Inside, I'm smoking,

like a fireplace burning

but no chimney,

Oh honey you've lit me.

They say they're scared of your flame,

of you burning like wildfire.

But that match in you is just the starter,

so screw them. Burn harder.

SWEETER DREAMS

I'm going to rest now,
and turn out the light;
and wish you sweetly a good night.

Of Lips and Lashes

By

Emily Armanios

Raw, real and emotion-charged, this collection of poetry encompasses the thoughts that have undoubtedly gone through the heads of every lover, fighter, and heartbroken soul.

These poems are creative and awe-inspiring, tackling harsher topics such as deception and loss whilst still including the lighter topics of family bonds and first loves.

Each individual poem incites a different image, a different passion, painting vivid pictures with the carefully-chosen words and perfectly flowing rhythm. It is a personal collection written to put the purest feelings into words, and seeks to creep into the minds and hearts of every reader.

Published by Kira Armanios

KArmanios

www.ingramcontent.com/pod-product-compliance
Lightning Source LLC
Chambersburg PA
CBHW070053100426
42740CB00013B/2838